MANAGING YOUR
MONEY AND FINANCES™

D1712457

# Making a Budget

Xina M. Uhl and Judy Monroe Peterson

Rosen
YA™

New York

Published in 2020 by The Rosen Publishing Group, Inc.
29 East 21st Street, New York, NY 10010

First Edition

**Library of Congress Cataloging-in-Publication Data**

Names: Uhl, Xina M., author. | Peterson, Judy Monroe, author.
Title: Making a budget / Xina M. Uhl and Judy Monroe Peterson.
Description: First edition. | New York: Rosen Publishing,
2020. | Series: Managing your money and finances | Includes
bibliographical references and index.
Identifiers: LCCN 2018048114| ISBN 9781508188551 (library
bound) | ISBN 9781508188544 (pbk.)
Subjects: LCSH: Budgets, Personal—Juvenile literature. |
Finance, Personal—Juvenile literature.
Classification: LCC HG179 .U335 2020 | DDC 332.024—dc23
LC record available at https://lccn.loc.gov/2018048114

*Manufactured in the United States of America*

# CONTENTS

# INTRODUCTION

**P**art of growing up involves taking responsibility for your own needs, like shelter, food, and clothing, and wants, like the latest video game or a top-of-the-line smartphone. As human beings, the things we want to buy can be endless. Yet the amount of money we have is not endless. How can we make sure we pay our bills every month and buy things we want as well? By using a budget.

Using a budget can help you reach your goals while also planning for unexpected expenses, like car repairs, medical bills, or a college tuition increase. A good budget takes into account your necessary bills, savings for the unexpected, and savings for goals, such as a new car or a big vacation.

When you first start to receive your own money, whether as an allowance from your parents or from a first job, it can be easy to spend it all at once. After all, you deserve to have fun. Why shouldn't you spend your money on pizza, a movie, and shopping

School can teach us many useful skills, but personal budgeting is usually not one of them. Yet this skill has a profound effect on the quality of your life.

for new clothes? Having a budget does not keep you from having fun. Setting up and maintaining a budget allows you to pay your bills, have a little extra for fun, and save for the future as well.

Knowing how to earn, spend, and save money are important money management skills that will serve you well for years to come. By learning and practicing these skills, you can master money management and that can lead you to becoming financially independent. Budgeting skills are also necessary to reach many of your goals in life.

By making and following a budget, you will understand what you earn, how you spend it, and how you can save it. A budget provides you with a summary of your current finances. You can then use this summary to make smart money choices. For example, you can determine if you have enough money to buy a car (sticker price and taxes) and operate it (fuel, insurance, and repairs).

Some people do not bother to make budgets, perhaps considering them too much work. Other people make budgets but do not stick to them. The problem with not making or not sticking to budgets is that you can easily lose track of where your money goes. A budget takes the guesswork out of managing your money.

Any good budget covers your income, expenses, and savings. Income is any money coming in. This can be earnings—money you receive for working—or money that you receive from someone, like an allowance or gift. Expenses are money going out, like bills you need to pay. Savings refers to money that you set aside to spend in the future.

If you don't have a budget, you will probably find yourself living from day to day. That means you might not have enough money for things you want now or in the future. A budget helps you meet small goals, like having enough money to join your friends for dinner at a fast-food restaurant. Larger goals, such as paying for an education, should also be a part of your budget. By taking control of your money with a budget, you are making a plan to accomplish important goals in your life.

# CHAPTER ONE

# Tracking Income and Expenses

**A** budget is made of different parts. The two major parts are your income and expenses. Income refers to any money you receive. The money you spend is known as expenses.

## A Money Tree

Wouldn't it be nice if money grew on trees, just like fruit? Then you could go outside and pick however much money you needed to buy what you wanted. That's not how the real world works, though. As a young person, you may receive money from family members and friends for your birthday or other special occasions.

Perhaps you earn some of the money that you spend. You might get a paycheck by working a job outside your home. Perhaps you work in a grocery store as a cashier or bagger, or maybe you work in a fast-food restaurant. When you receive your paycheck, you will see

While creating a budget may seem intimidating, remember that there are only two basics elements in it: your income and your expenses.

the gross pay, or the total amount earned before deductions are subtracted. Deductions are amounts that are withheld from, or taken out of, your gross pay. These include federal income tax, Social Security tax, and Medicare tax. Your state government might require that state income tax be withheld. The net pay is the amount of money you receive after all deductions have been subtracted.

Special employment laws apply to anyone under the age of eighteen who is working. To learn about the employment laws in your state, check with your school counselor. The laws restrict the number of hours a week you can work and the time of day you can work. Some kinds of jobs are off limits to minors as well. Your school counselor can help you figure out the rules in your state.

You can earn income in your neighborhood by doing odd jobs. Odd jobs could include babysitting, mowing lawns and other

Mowing neighbors' lawns can be a source of some income. You may even build up a steady stream of customers.

landscaping tasks, shoveling snow, and washing windows. You might get paid an allowance from your parents or guardians. Your allowance might be paid weekly, biweekly (every two weeks), or once a month. Sometimes allowances are given for doing chores around the house.

Sometimes, you might sell objects that you no longer want, such as video games or movies, for cash. In addition, you might be earning income from interest that is paid in a savings account. Banks pay interest on using money that is deposited, or put into, savings accounts. You might also get income by asking a parent or guardian for money to buy something.

Do you borrow money from friends or relatives? You might have money that you owe to someone or retail or credit card debt. Borrowed money, whether from a person or a retail or

**Take advantage of your loved ones' experience with good money management.**

credit card, is not income. Any borrowed money is a debt that must be repaid. You might not be able to pay your debt off at once. Talk to the person and agree to a plan to pay off your debt with regular payments. Set up and budget for a plan to pay off your debt with regular monthly payments.

## What Comes In

To make a budget, you need to know your income. Look at the sample average weekly income on page 11. To determine your weekly income, set up a worksheet in a word processing or spreadsheet program. Or use a notebook or sheet of paper. Write the title Average Weekly Income and the date. Then, make a table with two columns. Enter your sources of income and the net amounts for one week. Include income from all sources: gifts, jobs, allowances, and so on. To find your total income for that week, add all of your income. Round the money up to the nearest dollar.

# Budgeting Is Critical

Budgeting is a skill that many teens and adults lack. Not knowing how to make a budget—and stick to a budget—can create problems for anyone. A good budget always includes savings for emergencies. In 2018, a report by the Federal Reserve Board revealed that four in ten Americans are not able to cover a $400 emergency expense without selling something or borrowing the money from someone.

Bankrate.com's chief financial analyst Greg McBride commented about the report: "The finding that four in ten adults couldn't cover an unexpected $400 expense without selling something or borrowing money is troubling. Nothing is more fundamental to achieving financial stability than having savings that can be drawn upon when the unexpected occurs."

McBride recommends starting a savings habit by setting up automatic direct deposits from a paycheck to a savings account. The most important thing is to start a savings habit, no matter how small at first.

## Average Weekly Income, Week of January 9–15

| | |
|---|---|
| Paycheck, cashier job | $120.89 |
| Odd job, snow shoveling | $ 10.00 |
| Cash for birthday | $ 50.00 |
| Cash from Dad | $ 20.00 |
| Sold DVD | $ 5.00 |
| Actual Total: | $205.89 |
| Rounded Up: | $206.00 |

## What Goes Out

The next step in making a budget is to know what you currently buy. You need to know how much money you spend to buy goods or services, or you could be budgeting unrealistic amounts for your expenses. Keeping an expense record for a week will show you what you have bought that week. In turn, knowing these expenses will help you make your budget.

Look at the sample of a weekly expense record on page 13. To make an expense record, set up a worksheet in a word processing or spreadsheet program. Or use a notebook or sheets of paper clipped together. Enter the title Expense Record and the date. Then make a table with three columns. Enter the date you bought an item, the name of the item, and the cost. Include any expenses that you pay for by cash, check, credit card, or debit card. Keep track of all your expenses, including gas, bus or subway fares, clothing, shoes, jewelry, soda and candy, tickets to a movie, and so on. Jot down everything, even if the amount is less than a dollar.

Ask for and keep receipts for anything that you buy. Use your receipts to help you remember what you bought as you keep your expense record. You might want to keep your receipts in a large envelope, folder, or small box.

To help you keep track, fill out your expense record every time you buy something. Or fill out your expense record two or three times each day. For example, you might want to fill in your expenses after lunch, after supper, and before going to bed. At the end of the week, add up your expenses and write the total. Round the money up to the nearest dollar. Once you have your weekly expense record, look over your expenses and the total amount that you spent. Are you surprised at the total weekly cost for some of the items you bought, such as $13 in music downloads or $39 in food and snacks? Do you think you bought any unnecessary

# Sample Expense Record for Week of January 9–15

**Monday**

| | |
|---|---|
| Lunch at school | $ 5.00 |
| Soda | $ 2.00 |
| Gas for car | $40.00 |
| Haircut | $18.00 |

**Tuesday**

| | |
|---|---|
| Magazine | $ 5.00 |
| Gift for friend | $20.00 |
| Gum and soda | $ 3.00 |
| Music downloads | $ 3.00 |

**Wednesday**

| | |
|---|---|
| Baseball cap | $15.00 |
| Chips and soda | $ 3.00 |

**Thursday**

| | |
|---|---|
| Music downloads | $ 5.00 |

**Friday**

| | |
|---|---|
| Pizza, fries, shake | $18.00 |

**Saturday**

| | |
|---|---|
| DVD rental | $ 8.00 |
| Popcorn, soda | $ 8.00 |
| Jacket | $76.00 |

**Sunday**

| | |
|---|---|
| Music downloads | $ 5.00 |

| | |
|---|---|
| Total: | $234.00 |

things? Did you borrow money from a friend or relative so that you could buy something?

Now, you want to see if your weekly expenses match your weekly income. Subtract the total of your weekly expenses from the total of your weekly income. In the sample on page 11, the weekly income was $206. In the sample on page 13, the expenses for the same week were $234. The person overspent by $28.

When you subtract your expenses from your income, you can have three results. If the difference is zero, then you are balanced for that week. If the result is a positive number, then you have money left over. If your expenses are more than your income (a negative number or a minus sign), then you overspent. In all three

**Receipts can be a challenge to keep track of.
One option is to use a smartphone app like
Google Lens or Smart Receipt.**

cases, budgeting will help you manage your money now and in the future.

Keep your expense record for a second week or even longer. A monthly expense record will help you realize where your money is going. The more you see how you are spending your money, the easier it will be to manage your money.

## Separating Expenses

Look over your expenses again. In a word processing or spreadsheet file or on a sheet of paper, write categories to group your expenses. Your categories might include transportation, eating out, snacks and soda, entertainment, clothes and shoes, school supplies, gifts, savings, and others.

Go over your categories for your weekly expense record. What categories did you spend the most on? Are you surprised at the totals for some categories? Can you think of categories you might have missed? Now that you have tracked your income sources and expenses for a week or more, you are ready to make your budget.

# Myths and Facts

**Myth:** Budgeting is difficult.

**Fact:** A budget is straightforward. When you budget, you use basic math: adding, subtracting, multiplying, and dividing. By budgeting, you take control of your own finances and decide your own financial goals. You will make your life happier and easier by avoiding the stress of living from day to day or with debt.

**Myth:** Very few people budget.

**Fact:** Many people and families create and follow budgets. You might not know this because people might not talk about their budgets. In addition, governments, federal agencies, businesses, and organizations prepare and manage budgets. Whether a budget is for one person or for many people, money must be managed carefully.

**Myth:** Having a budget is restrictive—it keeps a person from buying the things that he or she wants.

**Fact:** A budget is a spending plan. Think of your spending plan as a road map for your finances. Your budget will help you plan your finances now and for your future. A budget will show you what you can afford to spend on things that you want. A budget can also help you achieve your money goals.

# CHAPTER TWO

# Your Monthly Budget

**A** budget is necessary because it helps you track your income and expenses. If you spend more money than you receive, you will quickly find yourself in trouble. Many people go into debt when they don't practice good budget skills.

Your budget will contain two sections: income and expenses. From your work in the previous chapter, you already have a clear idea of what amounts make up your weekly income and expenses. Now, you will make a budget for a month. As you make your budget, you will add more information to both sections. Then, you will compare your income and expenses and evaluate your results.

Think of a budget as a table with two sections. The first section is Net Income. The second section is Expenses. Note the two types of expenses, fixed and variable. Fixed expenses stay the same from month to month. Rent is an example of a fixed expense. Variable expenses, such as food and entertainment, change over time.

You can set up your budget on a personal finance app or on a financial website.

You can also use a word processing or spreadsheet program. If you would rather go low-tech, then make your budget in a notebook that is dedicated to that purpose. First, enter a title, such as Monthly Budget and a date. Next, make two sections. Label the top section Net Income. Label the bottom section Expenses. Make five columns in each section. You are ready to begin entering information into your monthly budget.

## Understanding Income

Making a budget begins with your income. You already know what your average net income is for one week. Now, determine your average net income for one month. In the Net Income section of your budget, enter your average sources of regular (ongoing) income and the amount for each income source for one month. Include your allowance and earnings from all jobs. If you are paid weekly, then multiply your net pay from your paycheck by 52, divide by 12, and enter that amount. If you are paid biweekly (every two weeks), then multiply your net pay by 26, divide by 12, and enter that amount.

Include other regular income, such as interest on savings accounts. You might get income from a savings account quarterly (every three months). To figure out this amount as monthly income, divide the interest by three. For example, if you get $30 every quarter as interest income, then divide $30 by three. You receive $10 every month as interest income.

Your income might vary from month to month. You might work more hours during the summer because you are not in

# Sample Monthly Budget

|  |  | Budget | Actual |
|---|---|---|---|
| Net Income | Avenge Pay from Job | $640 | $649 |
|  | Interest Income | $5 | $5 |
|  | Other | $0 | $0 |
| Total Monthly Income |  | $645 | $654 |
| Expenses |  |  |  |
| Fixed Expenses | Car Payment | $150 | $146 |
|  | Car Insurance | $205 | $205 |
|  | Cell Phone | $15 | $28 |
|  | Parking and Tolls | $12 | $18 |
|  | Others | $0 | $0 |
| Variable Expenses | School Expenses | $15 | $18 |
|  | Entertainment and Gifts | $40 | $48 |
|  | Transportation/Gas | $40 | $56 |
|  | Personal Items | $15 | $26 |
| Savings | Emergency Funds | $20 | $20 |
|  | Investments | $18 | $10 |
|  | Short-Term Saving (Jacket) | $10 | $5 |
|  | Medium-Term Saving (Travel) | $20 | $0 |
|  | Long-Term Saving (College) | $20 | $30 |
| Ongoing | Clothing and Shoes | $60 | $85 |
| Donation | Local Animal Shelter | $5 | $0 |
| Total Expenses/Saving/Donation |  | $645 | $695 |
| Income Minus Expenses |  | $0 | -$41 |

school. As a result, your income in the summer might be higher than in the winter. Use the lowest monthly income for your budget.

Do not include any uncertain sources of money as income. You cannot depend on unexpected income. Gifts of money, cash from selling things, money from odd jobs, or birthday and holiday gifts are not regular income sources.

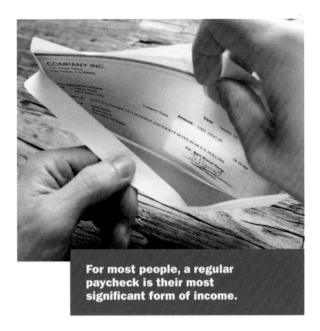

For most people, a regular paycheck is their most significant form of income.

Finish entering all regular sources of income for a month. Then, add all your income amounts. Enter this amount in Total Monthly Income.

## Calculating Expenses

The next part of a budget is your expenses and how much money you plan to spend on each expense. You already know your expenses for one week. To make your budget, look more closely at your monthly expenses.

Look over your weekly spending expenses from chapter 1. Think about your spending habits and financial goals. What are your spending priorities? What do you absolutely need? What are you saving for? How much do you plan to save in the short term and long term? How much do you need for future expenses, such

# Online Budgeting Tools

Some websites provide free budgeting tools. They might have chat rooms where you can share ideas about money with others. But be careful about sharing personal and financial information online. Do not give anyone your passwords or personal identification numbers (PINs). Protect your identity and money from internet ID theft. Look for and read the privacy statements on websites. Privacy statements might be on websites' homepages or in the About or FAQ section. Look for secure web pages. Signals that you have found one include a screen notice that you are in a secure website or a closed key in the bottom corner of the web page. Another sign is if "https" (hypertext transfer protocol secure) appears as the first letters of the internet address you are viewing, which means that you are using a site that transfers data securely over the internet.

It's a good idea to get in the habit of determining the security of whatever website you are on by checking the URL for "https."

as a new computer or college? Do you have an emergency fund? Do you share your money with causes that are important to you?

Review past bills and saved receipts to help you estimate some expenses. Also, look at records, cancelled checks, and credit card and bank statements. To plan for inflation, set your expense budget a little higher. Inflation is an increase in the price of goods or services that you buy. It makes things more expensive.

## Expenses That Don't Change

You must pay fixed expenses regularly. Fixed expenses might include car payments, auto insurance, and rent for an apartment.

One of the best habits you can get into is to keep track of the entries in your bank statement. Sometimes mistakes happen and it's best if you can catch them yourself.

Other fixed expenses might be cell phone bills, parking fees, public transportation fares, and dues.

You might have payments that are due once a year, such as a car license fee. To figure out an annual fee for your monthly budget, divide the annual fee by 12. Enter that amount in your budget. For example, divide an annual auto license fee of $192 by 12 to get a monthly amount of $16.

If you pay your auto insurance twice each year, then add the two payments to get the total. Divide the total by 12 to get the monthly amount. What is the monthly amount of two auto insurance payments of $616 and $627?

$616 + $627 = $1,243 (total amount)
$1,243 ÷ 12 = $104 (monthly amount)

Remember to round up to the nearest dollar.

## Expenses That Do Change

After paying for fixed expenses, you probably have money left over. You can use this disposable income to pay for variable, or nonfixed, expenses. Variable expenses typically change over time. Your variable expenses might include food, clothes and shoes, household and personal items, transportation and car upkeep, school expenses, entertainment and gifts, and other categories. What you actually spend on variable expenses might be different from what you have budgeted for. Be sure to include variable expenses in your budget. You might want to estimate your variable expenses. To arrive at realistic estimates, review your receipts, bills, online transactions, and other records from the past two or three months.

Variable expenses include savings and sharing, or donations you make to causes you believe in. Saving is putting money away for emergencies and short-term, medium-term, and long-term goals. A good budget includes an emergency fund. Each month, set money aside to prepare for unexpected events, like car repairs. You might want to set aside 5 percent of your monthly income for emergencies. For example, if your monthly income is $824, then multiply that amount by 5 percent: $824 × .05 = $41. Include $41 every month in your budget for emergencies.

Decide how much to set aside for your other savings goals. What financial goals are important to you now and in the future? When do you want to reach these goals? Include the amounts for savings in your budget. Saving regularly can help you reach goals such as buying a car or going on a vacation. To help you save, keep your bank accounts and any investment information up to date.

Having a healthy savings account makes unexpected expenses less painful.

Donating, or giving to causes, is another variable expense. Decide what causes are important to you. Then, decide how much money you want to set aside each month for sharing. Include that amount in your budget.

Once you have your total income and total expenses, balance your budget for the month. To balance your budget, subtract your expenses from your income. Do you have enough income to pay for your expenses? Do you have money left over? If it's a negative number, then you are spending more money than you have.

## Experimenting with Your Budget

If your income did not equal your expenses, then you are in need of a balanced budget. Check your expenses and income. Perhaps you did not include all your expenses, or you were unrealistic about your expenses. Maybe you did not include some monthly income, or you included an uncertain source of income.

If your total income and total expenses for the month are equal, then you have a balanced budget. A balanced budget is your goal. Usually, a balanced budget takes some time and practice to achieve.

You might want to make some changes to your monthly budget at this point. Or you might want to follow your budget for a month. At the end of the month, record your actual income and expenses. Find the difference between your budgeted income and expenses. Do you need to adjust your budget now? Your budget is a work in progress. Evaluating and adjusting your budget are important steps in managing your money.

# CHAPTER THREE

# Evaluating Your Budget

Perhaps you don't think much about whether to save or spend the money you receive. If that's the case, it's a mistake. By planning what to do with your money even before you receive it, you can begin to practice good money management. Be sure to get in the habit of saving while you are young—it will pay off in the years to come.

When you first set up your budget, you might forget to include some expenses and categories. You might be spending more on wants than needs (luxuries vs. necessities). If you have not planned and budgeted for your financial goals, then you might not be saving enough money. As a result, you might not reach your financial goals.

## The Difference Between Needs and Wants

Needs are things you must have, such as clothing and shoes. Wants are things you would like to have. A designer T-shirt

It's all too tempting to throw ideas of budgeting and saving out the window when you cash your paycheck, but it's a dangerous habit to get into.

or designer shoes are wants. You probably have ideas about needs and wants that are different from those of your friends. Transportation for work is a need. If you live in a city, to get to and from work, you might use the city bus, subway, or train. You would view a car for getting to work as a want. Your friend, however, might live in the country and not have access to public transportation. Your friend would view a car for getting/ to work as a need.

To make a realistic budget, decide what is important to you. Determine what things you could not live without and put them in your budget. Then, determine the wants that are most import-ant to you and include them.

Buying a car is a huge expense. If you decide to take the plunge, however, be sure to check out how functional the vehicle is, especially if it is used.

## What Are Your Spending and Saving Patterns?

Budgeting involves making spending and saving choices. How do you spend your money? How much money do you really need? What are you willing to give up to buy or save for what you want? Do you regularly save some money? Is investing money important to you?

By having a realistic budget for items like clothing, you can keep track of expenses more efficiently than if you just wing it.

To make a realistic budget, you need to know your spending and saving patterns. Your fixed expenses are known once you decide what you cannot live without. Subtract these needs from your income. The money remaining is what you can spend on your wants.

Perhaps you have not budgeted enough for savings. Look at your variable expenses. Are you downloading songs to your smartphone every week? Downloading music is probably a want, not a need. Could you live happily if you downloaded fewer songs every other week or even once a month? This change provides more savings for your needs or financial goals.

If your needs are greater than your income, then consider increasing your income. One option is to work odd jobs to supplement your income. You might decide to babysit two Fridays

Having a grocery list is one of the best ways to avoid impulse buys. Another is to make sure you don't go to the store when you're hungry.

every month. You would gain two financial benefits: extra income and not spending money on those Friday evenings.

Grow good money habits. Save first when you get paid. Put your money into savings to reach your financial goals. If you have money for wants, then budget for occasional impulse buying.

To help you manage your money, make a list of what you need before you shop. Stick to your list when shopping.

## Setting Financial Goals

The most important part of managing your money is determining what is important to you. First, determine your short-term (one month to twelve months), medium-term (thirteen months to twenty-four months), and long-term (twenty-five months to sixty months) financial goals. Set goals based on your values, not on what your friends or others have or want. Make your goals specific and measurable: "Save $25 a week for twenty weeks until I have enough money to buy a computer." Put your financial goals in writing to make them more concrete. Next, prioritize your goals. Then, choose the goals you want to work toward.

Say a short-term goal is to buy a computer that costs $1,000 in five months. If you budget $25 a week, then you will not make your goal: $25 × 20 weeks = $500. Instead, you decide to save $50 for twenty weeks. Then, you will reach your goal: $50 × 20 weeks = $1,000. Or you might decide to wait longer and save $25 a week for 10 months: $25 × 40 weeks = $1,000.

A medium-term goal might be to put 10 percent of your income into savings for college. Look over your budget. Perhaps you can reach this goal by cutting your entertainment expenses by 10 percent.

To reach your financial goals, you need to save money. You might also want to support your community or organizations that are important to you. Think about support that you can offer to organizations like the American Red Cross, American Heart Association, Humane Society of the United States, or an environmental organization. Perhaps you might want to offer support to your public library, a local animal shelter, a local community center, or your faith community.

## Adjusting as Needed

Evaluating and adjusting your budget are important steps. Review your budget after one month to see if it is helping you reach your financial goals. You might need to adjust categories.

Continue evaluating your budget monthly, even if it is balancing. Your financial goals, needs, and wants will change over time. Your income will probably change. Your expenses might also change. Keeping your budget up to date is vital to having your budget work for you.

A successful budget is very useful, but it can take time to create. Budgeting might be a new habit for you. It takes time and practice to learn something new. Here are some things to keep in mind when making a budget:

1. Include an emergency fund in your budget to prepare for unexpected events. Perhaps your car won't start. After it is towed to an auto repair shop, you learn that your car needs a new alternator. You might use your entire emergency fund to pay for the tow and repairs. Reset your financial goals and adjust your budget to build your emergency fund up again.

2. You may have randomly decided which categories to cut down when making your budget. At first, you might not know if the amounts will work. As you work with and evaluate your budget, you may need to increase the amounts in certain categories, such as savings or gas. Decrease the amounts in nonessential categories. For example, cut out eating at fast-food restaurants for one month. Save that money to buy a new printer or add to your emergency fund.

3. Have you set realistic financial goals? Perhaps you are saving to buy a car. According to your budget, it will take eighteen months to reach this goal. Sticking with your budget for

so long might be difficult. To help you reach your goals, set small milestones along the way. Reward yourself at each milestone. You might buy yourself a video game if you do not eat at fast-food restaurants for a

Although the cost of treats like this one can seem small, they add up quickly unless you keep track of them.

month. Little rewards can help you stick to your budget.

4. Do you have some money for fun in your budget? Slashing your entertainment dollars too much might set you up to fail. You might overspend if you feel deprived. If your budget is tight, though, you might have to limit your fun money to $20 or less per month.

5. Write down your financial goals. Put them next to your cash, credit, or debit card in your wallet or purse. Look over your goals before you buy something to help you stick to your budget. You might avoid stores in which you have overspent in the past.

Adjusting and evaluating your budget takes some time. Are you taking enough time? Aim to work on your budget once a month or try shorter blocks of time. Work for five minutes each day or thirty minutes every week. Once you reach a large financial goal, set a new goal or goals and adjust your budget. Over time, your needs will change, and so will your budget. Remember to include savings in your expenses because it is money put away for future expenses.

# CHAPTER FOUR

# Saving Now and Later

**B**udgeting is all about balance. You never want to spend so much that you run out of funds entirely. Learning how to save effectively will keep you from overspending and help you set financial goals for the future.

## The Value of Saving

Saving helps you care for yourself both in the short term and the long term. You might have expenses you did not expect. Or you might want money to buy something special. If you have budgeted for savings, then you will have that money when you need it.

Start a savings plan. Look again at your short-term, medium-term, and long-term financial goals from chapter 3. When you budget for your goals, put Savings as your first expense. Make saving a habit by always paying yourself first.

When you open your first bank account, it is a good idea to take someone along who can answer questions. Bankers themselves should be a good source of helpful information.

How much should you save? A good rule is to save 10 percent of your income. You might be able to save more depending on your financial goals.

Setting up an emergency fund is an important short-term savings goal. Use emergency funds to pay for unexpected repairs on your car, for example. You probably also have some fun short-term goals, such as buying sports gear, a bike, or visiting a theme park.

Medium-term and long-term financial goals are goals further in the future. These goals might include saving money for college, a vacation, or a new car. Future financial goals generally require more money than short-term goals. To meet future goals, you typically save small amounts of money over a long period of time.

## Keeping Your Money Secure

Are you saving money by hiding it in an old sock? A better idea is to start a savings account at a bank. By putting your money away, you won't be as tempted to spend it. You can also watch your savings grow because banks pay you interest for keeping your money. Interest is paid as a percentage of the amount that you deposit. You can set up one savings account. Or you might want to set up three savings accounts to separate long-term, medium-term, and short-term savings goals.

Savings products offered by banks are safe places to put your money. The federal government through the Federal Deposit Insurance Corporation (FDIC) insures bank deposits up to $250,000 per bank. Your savings are available to you when you need them. Savings products offered by banks include savings accounts, money market accounts, certificates of deposit (CDs), and US savings bonds.

Money market accounts require a large deposit and a large minimum balance. Money market accounts earn more interest than a regular savings account. CDs require that you deposit money for a specific amount of time, such as six months or a year. CDs earn more interest than money market and savings accounts. You pay a large fee if you take out your money early from a CD.

**Since the FDIC's founding in 1933, no depositor has ever lost any money.**

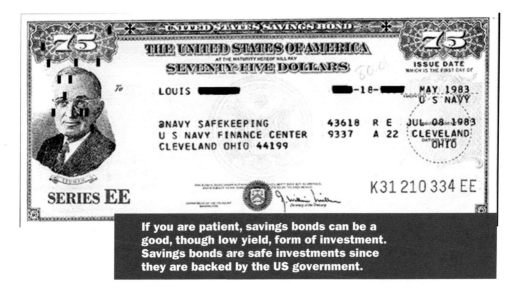

If you are patient, savings bonds can be a good, though low yield, form of investment. Savings bonds are safe investments since they are backed by the US government.

When you buy a US savings bond, you pay half its face value. A $100 savings bond would cost you $50. When the bond matures in twenty years, you can cash it in for its face value of $100. Some savings bonds earn interest after they mature.

## The Magic of Compounding

The key to saving is to make your money work for you through compounding. With compounding, you earn interest on the money that you save and on the interest the money earns. The power of compounding comes with time. The sooner you start saving, the more your money can work for you.

Say that you buy a can of soda for $1 every day for a year. That adds up to $365. Instead, imagine that you put that $365 into a savings account earning 5 percent per year. You would have $383 at the end of one year. In five years, your total would be $466. At the end of thirty years, your total would be $1,578. Even a small amount of savings can add up to big money because of compounding over time.

The stock market is a high energy, and high risk, institution. However, it is one that can earn investors a lot of money.

## Sound Investments

You can make your money grow by investing in stocks, bonds, mutual funds, or other money tools. Unlike bank savings, the federal government does not insure invested money. You have a higher risk of losing your money by investing than by savings. So why might you want to invest? You have the opportunity to earn more money with investments than with savings.

You might invest by buying stocks of a company. If the value of the stock goes up, then the company pays you money when you sell the stock. A company might also pay you dividends, which are the part of a company's profit paid to its stockholders. The stock value depends on how well the company is doing, how much people will pay for the stock, and the world economy. If the company does poorly, then you might lose some or all of your investment.

Another investment is bonds. A public company or a local, state, or national government might sell bonds to raise money. When you buy bonds, an organization pays you interest on your money. It also promises to return your money on a set due date, perhaps in ten years. Bonds generally are less risky than stocks.

Mutual funds are another option for investing. A mutual fund is a pool of money run by trained investment professionals. The mutual fund managers invest in a mix of stocks, bonds, and other items. Every mutual fund has a different level of risk and opportunities to earn money.

You might decide to join an investment club, which is often offered in schools. In these clubs, a group of people make decisions on investing. They pool their money to make investments. The group votes to buy or sell stocks, bonds, mutual funds, or other items.

## Cash and Credit

Many teens keep their money in both a checking account and a savings account. You write a check to pay for something with

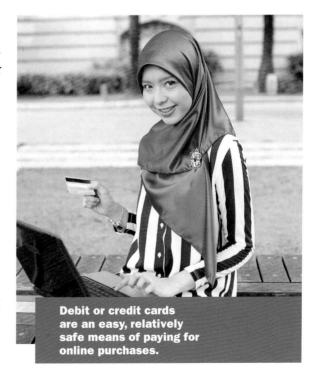

Debit or credit cards are an easy, relatively safe means of paying for online purchases.

money in your checking account. You can write paper checks or use online checks. Checks are safer to carry and send than cash.

An automated teller machine (ATM) card typically comes with your bank account. Using an ATM card and machine, you can make deposits to or get money from your bank accounts. Some banks charge a fee for every use of an ATM or for not using an ATM associated with your bank.

Using debit cards or credit cards are other ways to pay for goods and services. When you use a debit card, you pay now. A store takes money from your checking or savings account immediately to pay for something. Some debit cards have monthly fees. Others charge a fee for each use. Banks charge overdraft fees if you use your debit card without having enough money deposited in your account.

Unlike debit cards, you pay later with credit cards. A credit card lets you borrow money. When you use a credit card, the store gets the money you owe from the bank. After about a month, the bank totals your credit card charges and sends you a bill. You can pay the whole bill, or you can pay some of what you owe and pay the rest later. The bank charges interest on the amount you do not pay back.

Some people continue to put new charges on their credit cards and never pay the entire amount. Over time, they could owe a lot of money to their bank. This debt could affect their credit score, a number that shows the credit risk of a person. A person with a low credit score might have difficulty getting a loan from a bank for school tuition or to buy a car.

Sometimes, you might find that saving is difficult. You might be tempted to withdraw your savings to buy something you want now instead of saving toward a future goal. Keep your financial goals in mind. Stick to your savings plan. Wise spending can help you keep more of your money for savings.

# 10 Great Questions to Ask a Financial Adviser

1. How much time does it take to set up a budget? Should I do it weekly or monthly?

2. How much money should I keep in an emergency fund?

3. Should I save my money in a savings account, a money market account, a CD, savings bonds, or some combination of these?

4. When should I use a debit card or a credit card?

5. How many credit cards should I have?

6. How do I establish a good credit score?

7. Should I take out a loan or pay cash to buy a car?

8. What are the best types of investments for me: stocks, bonds, or mutual funds?

9. Are collectibles, such as gold or silver coins, a good investment?

10. Should I ask a third party to review my budget once a year? If yes, who should do it?

# CHAPTER FIVE

# Spending and Your Budget

**S**aving is a necessary practice if you want to make wise choices with your money. But after you have a plan in order—one that you can stick with—it's time to pay your expenses. Set your spending priorities by determining your needs from your wants.

## Spend Smart

After following your budget for a month or longer, do you usually spend more than your income? You have two ways to deal with this. One option is to increase your income. However, you might not be able to work more hours. Besides work, you need time for school and studying, family, recreation, and other activities that are important to you.

A second option is to reduce your spending. Practice discipline and control in your spending habits. For costly items, make buying decisions based on careful thought and research. Avoid impulse buying. Keep your receipts so that you can return unnecessary items.

Try to be thoughtful about spending. Learn to do this by removing your emotions from your money. Say you are out with friends and see a tempting pair of shoes in a store. Before buying, ask yourself if these shoes are a necessity or a want. If you made a list of ne-

Make sure you compare items' prices since they can vary widely.

cessities, would the shoes be on your list? Would your life change for the better if you owned these shoes? If the answer is no, then do not buy them.

You might find it difficult to pass on the latest cell phone if all of your friends have it. Think about your personal values, though. Ignore advertisers and the opinions of your peers. Although peers can influence you, remember that you make your own spending decisions.

Be realistic about your spending strengths and weaknesses. Can you go to a mall without buying something? Do you always buy something at your favorite store? Avoid these places until you can limit your spending. You might want to sleep on a large buying decision. Another method is to write what you want to buy on a piece of paper. Put the paper away for a week or longer. Time might blunt your desire to buy the item.

Window shopping can be a fun way to spend time, but it can also end up costing you plenty.

## Make Wise Habits

To gain more expense money, look at your habits. If you buy soda or coffee every day, consider drinking water instead and buying a water bottle to fill it up with from the fountains at school for free. Bring your own juice or snacks in reusable containers from home. Limit sodas and coffees.

Plan ahead when you drive, and group small trips together to use gas efficiently. Keep your car tuned up and tires inflated for better gas mileage. Using a carpool or taking public transportation may save you money, too.

Showing your student ID might save you money on movies, transportation, and meals. Many programs have discounts for students. If you are not sure, ask about student discounts.

Shop at used clothing and thrift stores for clothes, accessories, furniture, and other items. Before you buy, ask yourself: What will you do with the item? Where will you store it? What are the cleaning costs? Are repairs costly?

Comparison shopping helps you stay within your budget and live within your means. As a comparison shopper, you want to buy high-quality items at the lowest price. As you research items, ask

Transportation costs can be significant, so make sure you think carefully about whether you need your own vehicle or not.

yourself: Do you need a brand name? If yes, then what brand? Where might you buy the item? Do you need to buy now or later? Can the items be new or used? Do you need to earn more money to buy any items? Use comparison shopping websites to evaluate prices.

## Fees Can Creep Up on You

Do you need to adjust your spending to avoid bank fees? Banks often charge fees on everything from using their online bill-paying service to having a negative account balance. You might be charged a fee if your balance is negative for even a few minutes. Some banks charge a monthly fee for checking accounts. Others do not charge a monthly fee if you maintain a specified minimum

# Comparing Automobile Prices

Use comparison shopping to help you decide on the type of car that you can afford. First, list the costs of owning a car. Your list might include car payments, gas, insurance, repairs, and license. Next, check the values and repair history of cars that you want to buy. Read car reviews and car ratings. Then, ask an insurance agent for insurance costs on cars that you might want. The type of car influences the cost of insurance.

When it comes time to start looking at cars in your area, you will want to visit a number of dealerships to see what is available and to test-drive cars to see how they handle. Buying a car in person can be a stressful experience, though, as car salespeople are experienced at pressuring buyers into spending more than they want for extras that they may not need. Another option is to use an app like TrueCar. This app lists a number of vehicles from across the country. You pay the price listed, with no haggling. You can search for new and used cars and even get a trade-in option for your old car.

balance. Banks charge a stop-payment fee to stop a check or an automatic bill payment.

ATM fees can quickly add up. Banks might charge a fee every time you use an ATM. If you use an ATM that belongs to another bank, your bank and the company that owns the ATM may both charge you fees.

Unless you keep track of your income and expenses, you may find that bank fees and nonsufficient-funds charges eat up your balance.

If you spend more than you have in your account, your balance will be negative. Your bank will charge nonsufficient-funds (NSF) fees for every check or debit transaction that you make. The company will also charge you a fee. You will still owe the company the amount on the check or in the debit transaction.

## Looking for Bargains

Everyone likes to get a bargain or the best value on something. To determine what items are bargains, compare both price and quality. If you compare a single item at different stores, the item with the lower price is likely the better buy. Do a little math to find the better price on multiple items in a package.

For example, which is the better bargain: a two-pack of socks for $4.99 or a four-pack of socks for $7.99? Divide the cost by the amount to find the price per unit (pairs of socks):

$4.99 ÷ 2 = $2.50 per unit
$7.99 ÷ 4 = $2.00 per unit
The four-pack of socks is a better bargain.

Along with price, compare quality to determine the value. Which pair of socks is the better value: the thick two-pack or the thin four-pack? Thick socks last longer than thin socks. The two-pack socks are the better value.

Stores often put items on sale to entice people to buy them. If a pair of $30 jeans are discounted 20 percent, then how much are they? To find the answer, change 20 percent to a decimal, multiply the price by the discount, and subtract the discount from the price:

20% = .20
$30 × .20 = $6
$30 − $6 = $24
The jeans cost $24.

Pay attention to sales when you are shopping.
The savings can be significant.

Sometimes, stores further discount items. You might see a sign that reads "Take an additional 15 percent off" on $30 jeans that have already been discounted 20 percent. How much are the jeans? The discount is not the sum of the two percents added together (20% + 15% = 35%). To find the discounted price, figure each discount separately:

$30 × .20 = $6
$30 − $6 = $24 (price of jeans discounted 20 percent)

$24 × .15 = $3.60
$24 − $3.60 = $20.40 (price of jeans discounted 20 percent, plus another 15 percent discount)
　　The jeans cost $20.40.

Be aware of bait-and-switch methods. For instance, a store might entice you with great bargains. Once you are in the store, you are told the items are not available. Only similar and more costly items are for sale. This is deceptive advertising. Some car dealers use the bait-and-switch method. They might advertise a new car for $10,000 (bait). When you get to the car lot, however, the salespeople say that all of those cars are gone. Instead, they have similar cars that cost more (switch).

## Your Rights and Responsibilities

As a consumer of goods and services, you have certain rights and responsibilities. Four basic consumer rights are the right to safety, the right to be informed, the right to choose, and the right to be heard. Different agencies and organizations protect and help consumers with complaints. These include consumer affairs bureaus, media action programs, private consumer groups, licensing boards, and government services.

Government agencies include the Consumer Product Safety Commission (CPSC), which protects consumers against harmful products. The CPSC can ban or recall dangerous products. The Federal Trade Commission (FTC) prevents the unfair, false, or deceptive advertising of goods and services. The Food and Drug Administration (FDA) ensures that manufacturers' medicines are labeled, safe, and effective for their intended use.

Some companies are reputable, and some are not. Federal and state agencies cannot check all companies that sell in malls, in catalogs, on television, over the telephone, and on the web. As a consumer, you are responsible for researching the safety of products. Report any consumer fraud. You have a responsibility to complain when necessary and to make sure your complaints are dealt with fairly.

Sometimes, budgets can fail. If your budget is not working, look it over to see if you have unrealistic expenses. Have you forgotten some items or expenses? Do you have a written budget? Are you spending enough time working with your budget? Perhaps you have forgotten to budget money to do some fun things.

A good budget is geared toward your goals and is based on your needs and wants. You can change your budget if it is not working or if you have large changes in your life, such as getting a car. Your budget is an important tool for your financial well-being now and in the future.

# GLOSSARY

**bond** A promise to pay a certain amount on a certain date, issued by a company or government, to borrow money.

**budget** A plan for how to spend and save your money.

**certificate of deposit (CD)** A type of savings in which money is deposited for a certain period of time to earn a specific rate of interest.

**checking account** A bank account that allows the person to take out money, pay bills, or buy things by writing checks.

**comparison shopping** Researching brands to buy the highest quality at the lowest price.

**credit** An agreement in which someone buys something now and promises to pay for it later.

**credit score** A number that indicates a person's credit risk.

**deductions** Amounts withheld, or taken out of gross pay, such as federal and income taxes, Social Security tax, and Medicare tax.

**dividend** Portion of a company's profits paid to stockholders.

**earnings** Money received for doing work.

**expenses** Goods and services that people pay for with their money.

**fixed expenses**  Expenses that stay the same and must be paid from month to month, such as rent.

**gross pay**  The total amount earned before deductions are subtracted.

**income**  Money earned for doing work or received from savings, investments, or gifts.

**interest**  Money that banks pay for using money deposited in accounts.

**investing**  The risking of money and time to get more money in return.

**loan**  A sum of money borrowed for a certain amount of time.

**mutual fund**  An investment run by professionals in which people pool their money to buy stocks, bonds, and other items.

**overdraft fee**  A payment for having a negative balance in an account.

**savings account**  A bank account in which money is deposited for safekeeping.

**savings bonds**  Bonds issued by the federal government sold at half their face value.

**stock**  An investment in the ownership of a company.

**transaction**  Any business, such as a deposit or withdrawal, done with a bank.

**variable expenses**  Expenses that vary from month to month.

# FOR MORE INFORMATION

Canadian Bankers Association
Box 348
Commerce Court West
199 Bay Street, 30th Floor
Toronto, ON M5L 1G2
Canada
(800) 263-0231
Website: http://www.cba.ca
Twitter: @CdnBankers
The association provides information for teens to learn
    about money, budgeting, credit, investments, goal
    setting, and banking in Canada.

Certified Financial Planner Board
1425 K Street NW, #800
Washington, DC 20005
(800) 487-1497
Website: http://www.letsmakeaplan.org
Email: mail@CFPBoard.org
Facebook: @CFPLetsMakeAPlan
Twitter: @CFPBoard
The board offers personal financial planning
    information. Search the website for local certified
    financial planners.

Consumer Federation of America
1620 I Street NW, Suite 200

Washington, DC 20006
(202) 387-6121
Website: http://www.consumerfed.org
Facebook: @ConsumerFederationofAmerica
Twitter: @ConsumerFed
This group is an advocacy, research, and education
organization providing information and resources on
personal finances, including money management
and budgeting.

Federal Deposit Insurance Corporation (FDIC)
550 17th Street NW
Washington, DC 20429-9990
(877) ASK-FDIC [275-3342]
Website: http://www.fdic.gov
Facebook and Twitter: @FDICgov
An independent agency of the US government, the
FDIC protects people against the loss of deposits.
The agency also provides information on deposit
insurance, shopping for financial services,
understanding consumer rights, and avoiding
financial fraud.

Financial Literacy and Education Commission
C/O Office of Financial Education Department of
the Treasury
1500 Pennsylvania Avenue NW
Washington, DC 20220
(888) MY-MONEY (696-6639)
Website: http://www.mymoney.gov
The commission offers a variety of information on money
management and budgeting.

Financial Planners Standards Council
902–375 University Avenue
Toronto, ON M5G 2J5
Canada
(800) 305-9886
Email: inform@fpsc.ca
Facebook: @FPSC.Canada
Twitter: @FPSC_Canada
The council provides information and resources for
    teens on personal finance, budgeting, savings,
    investments, and more.

Jump$tart
1001 Connecticut Avenue NW, Suite 640
Washington, DC 20036
(202) 846-6780
Email: info@jumpstart.org
Website: http://www.jumpstart.org
Facebook and Twitter: @natljumpstart
The site offers information on budgeting, money
    management, setting goals, credit, and investing.
    Visit its clearinghouse to find a list of recommended
    books and other materials, CDs, DVDs, videos,
    and websites.

National Council on Economic Education
1140 Avenue of the Americas
New York, NY 10036
(800) 338-1192
Website: http://www.ncee.net
Facebook: @councilforeconed
Twitter: @council4econed

The council provides a personal finance website for teens at www.italladdsup.org, which covers budgeting, goal setting, credit, saving, and investing.

National Endowment for Financial Education
1331 17th Street, Suite 1200
Denver, CO 80202
(303) 741-6333
Website: http://www.nefe.org
This organization offers information and resources on money management, budgeting, setting financial goals, and more.

US Department of the Treasury
1500 Pennsylvania Avenue SW
Washington, DC 20220
(202) 622-2000
Website: http://home.treasury.gov
Facebook and Twitter: @ustreasury
The Treasury Department monitors and manages the overall state of the US economy. Its website includes the latest information on various types of bonds issued by the federal government, among other types of financial information.

# FOR FURTHER READING

Blohm, Craig E. *Teen Guide to Credit and Debt.* San Diego,
    CA: ReferencePoint Press, Inc., 2017.
Hardyman, Robyn. *Understanding Income and Savings.*
    New York, NY: Rosen Publishing, 2018.
Hardyman, Robyn. *Understanding Money Goals and
    Budgeting.* New York, NY: Rosen Publishing, 2018.
Hardyman, Robyn. *Understanding Stocks and Investing.*
    New York, NY: Rosen Publishing, 2018.
McGuire, Kara. *Making Money Work: The Teens' Guide
    To Saving, Investing, and Building Wealth.* North
    Mankato, MN: Capstone Young Readers, 2015.
McGuire, Kara. *The Teen Money Manual: A Guide to Cash,
    Credit, Spending, Saving, Work, Wealth, and More.* North
    Mankato, MN: Capstone Young Readers, 2015.
Minden, Cecelia. *Living on a Budget.* Ann Arbor, MI: Cherry
    Lake Publishing, 2016.
Nagle, Jeanne. *Money, Banking, and Finance.* New York,
    NY: Rosen Publishing, 2018.
Schlesinger, Emily, and Jennifer Liss. *Managing
    Money.* Costa Mesa, CA: Saddleback Educational
    Publishing, 2017.
Weeks, Marcus, and Derek Braddon. *Heads Up Money.*
    New York, NY: DK Publishing, 2016.

# BIBLIOGRAPHY

Bahney, Anna. "40% Of Americans Can't Cover a $400 Emergency Expense." CNNMoney, May 22, 2018. http://money.cnn.com/2018/05/22 /pf/emergency-expenses-household-finances /index.html.

Bodnar, Janet. *Raising Money Smart Kids: What They Need to Know About Money and How to Tell Them.* New York, NY: Kaplan Business, 2005.

Ellis, Megan. "6 of the Best Apps to Scan, Track, and Manage Receipts." MUO, December 3, 2018. https://www.makeuseof.com/tag/7-best-apps-scan -track-manage-receipts.

FDIC. "Federal Deposit Insurance Corporation." Retrieved October 21, 2018. http://www.fdic.gov/deposit /covered/notinsured.html.

FDIC. "When a Bank Fails - Facts for Depositors, Creditors, and Borrowers." July 28, 2014. https://www.fdic.gov/consumers/banking/facts.

Federal Deposit Insurance Corporation. "How to Ace Your First Test Managing Real Money in the Real World." *FDIC Consumer News*, Spring 2008, pp. 5–6.

Federal Deposit Insurance Corporation. "What to Know Before Declaring Your Financial Independence." *FDIC Consumer News*, Spring 2008, pp. 6–7.

Godfrey, Neale S., and Carolina Edwards. *Money Doesn't Grow on Trees: A Parent's Guide to Raising Financially Responsible Children.* New York, NY: Fireside, 2006.

GSA Office of Citizen Services and Communications. *Consumer Action Handbook*. Washington, DC: Federal Citizen Information Center, 2008.

Invester.gov. "Savings Bonds." Retrieved December 8, 2018. https://www.investor.gov/introduction-investing/basics/investment-products/savings-bonds.

MetLife Consumer Education Center and American Association of Individual Investors. *Building Financial Freedom*. New York, NY: MetLife, 2006.

Money Instructor. "Sample Monthly Household Budget." Retrieved October 19, 2018. http://content.moneyinstructor.com/437/sample-budget.html.

Office of Investor Education and Advocacy. *Get the Facts on Savings and Investing*. Washington, DC: U.S. Securities and Exchange Commission, 2007.

Orman, Suze. *The Money Book for the Young, Fabulous & Broke*. New York, NY: Riverhead Trade, 2007.

# INDEX

# ABOUT THE AUTHORS

**Xina M. Uhl** has authored a variety of books for young people, in addition to textbooks, teacher's guides, lessons, and assessment questions. When she is not writing or reading, she enjoys travel, photography, and hiking with her dogs. Her blog features her travel adventures and latest fiction projects.

**Judy Monroe Peterson** holds two master's degrees and is the author of numerous educational books for young people. She is a former technical, health care, and academic librarian and college faculty member; a research scientist; and a curriculum editor with more than twenty-five years of experience. She has taught courses at 3M, the University of Minnesota, and Lake Superior College. Currently, she is a writer and editor of K–12 and post–high school curriculum materials on a variety of subjects, including life skills.

# PHOTO CREDITS